Needlers
of Hull

By
Raymond Needler

HUTTON PRESS
1993

Published by The Hutton Press Ltd.,
130 Canada Drive, Cherry Burton,
Beverley, East Yorkshire HU17 7SB.

Typeset and Printed by
Image Colourprint Ltd.,
Anlaby, Hull.

ISBN 1 872167 55 1

CONTENTS

Page

Introduction 4

A Note on Sources 5

Acknowledgements 5

The Early Years 7

Private Life 9

The Company from 1900 10

The Move into Chocolate Production 12

Family Life from 1900 14

The Completion of the Chocolate Factory 16

The 1920's 16

The Products 17

Transport of Goods to Customers 18

The Depression 19

Needlers Musical Society 20

The Business After Fred Needler's Death 21

The Company from 1940 22

Appendix 1: Table of Turnover and Profit 1909-1939 23

Appendix 2: Long Service Employees 24

INTRODUCTION

This is the story of how my grandfather, Fred Needler, started from nothing to build up a business which in 40 years had become one of the largest employers in the city of Hull.

I have deliberately kept the story short, and the main part of the book is taken up with the many photographs and pictures from catalogues which have been kept.

I am often asked why the company was based in Hull; the answer is simply that Fred lived here. Like many businesses where there are no special needs of climate, transport or bulk materials, the enterprise is the result of the ability of the founder.

The photographs run out in the 1930's, so I have summarised the story up to the present time for completeness. The business is still in production on the same Sculcoates Lane site, though largely in new single storey extensions on the Sculcoates Lane side of the original buildings. It is now owned by the largest Norwegian food group, NORA SA.

Boiled sweets and toffees are still made under the Needler name, together with sales to the main supermarket groups with their own brand names, and there is a very large export business in addition.

RAYMOND NEEDLER
July 1993.

4

A NOTE ON SOURCES

Most of the old letters and other documents which the company kept on file dating from before 1939 were stored in the office loft, and were destroyed at the beginning of the 1939 war to avoid being a fire hazard in air raids.
My information comes mainly from the old and rather sketchy minute books which run from 1902, and the Private Ledger, which had the annual summary of figures transferred to it.
A booklet was produced in 1936 to record "50 years of progress", and this gives an outline of the history, which I have been able to fill out. I also have Fred Needler's personal cash books, and a note book he wrote during his visit to the USA in 1926. Fortunately the old photographs were kept in several boxes in the factory, although few of them were labelled; the captions are my own additions.

ACKNOWLEDGEMENTS

I have been supplied with the details on the photographs of vans by Ian Gibb, who has been working on the history of vehicle bodies produced by Barnaby Brothers.
My chief thanks must go to my wife Joan, who supported me during the 35 years I worked with the company, and has now given much help and encouragement with this book.

Frederick Needler

The Early Years

Frederick Needler was born at Arnold, a village near Skirlaugh in the East Riding of Yorkshire on 12th December 1864.

In fact, the family name is recorded on his birth certificate as Needley, and this name is also used on his father's marriage certificate, which tells us that George Needley, farmer of Aldbrough age 25 married Jane Duke of Mason Street, Hull on 7 April 1860, at Sculcoates. Going further back, George's father was Joseph Needley, also a farmer who married Sarah Winter at Owthorne, Withernsea in 1832.

The name changes to Needler on documents after 1865. Which name is correct is now uncertain, as George has signed the wedding certificate in a confident hand as Needley. However, most of the many other families still living in the Hull area with the Needler name are direct descendants of a different Joseph Needler who was a farmer at Easington, which is close to Aldbrough, and I have little doubt that the two families will have a common ancestry. There were four children of the marriage:

Selina, born September 1861 (married name Clifton, also Needley on the birth record).
Frederick, born December 1864.
John Henry, born 1870.
Lucy, born between late 1871 and 1873 (married name Buffey).

I do not know when the family moved to Hull; there is a baptism registered at Skirlaugh for Selina, but not for Fred. There was a steady drift from the country into the towns at this time and George would be looking for a safer job, with a family to support.

The 1871 census return shows the family living in Argyle Street, St John's Wood, which was the area between Pearson Park and Cottingham Road in modern Hull. George is shown as James Needler, head of household, wife Jane, and three children, Sleanne (sic), Frederick and Henry; places of birth of all are given as Hull. The Census taker wrote down what he was told, as often happened. The useful information is that the occupation of James/George is shown as colour maker, which implies that he was now employed in one of the paint factories in the Sculcoates area. I was confused by the residence in Argyle Street for some time, as the present street of that name is off Anlaby Road, and could not be in St. John's Wood. However a Hull directory of that time shows two Argyle Streets, the other one being off Queen's Road, which fits very nicely; it was renamed Maple Street in the 1880s.

Unfortunately, George Needler got typhoid, which was widespread in Hull in the nineteenth century, and died in their house on 27th September 1872, aged 37.

There must have been some money in the family, as Hull had a plentiful supply of very cheap housing, but of a dreadful standard around the centre of the city. However, the Queen's Road area was just being developed, and this would be new housing on the edge of the green fields, and rather more expensive. The family of four children did not fall into destitution on the death of George, although family rumour has it that Jane took in washing.

Fred went to St. John's school (presumably St. John's at Newland), but must have left as soon as he could, in order to earn. He got his first job in a tea and coffee warehouse in High Street about 1878. The 1881 census shows the family still at 163 Argyle Street; Jane is described as a laundress, Selina as a dressmaker and Fred as a Grocer's apprentice. He must have been good at figures, as at the age of 18 he moved to become a book-keeper to Edward Buckton as the result of a chance meeting by his mother. Mr. Buckton had a small manufacturing confectionery business at the corner of Midland Street and Osborne Street just south of Paragon Station.

Mr. Buckton's business ran into financial difficulties, and the plant was offered to Fred for £100, comprising two stoves, some slabs, rollers and basic utensils for the manufacture of boiled sweets. His mother had this amount as her savings and bought the equipment for Fred, who took premises in Anne Street nearby and started off for himself in 1886. An article in the _Hull Daily Mail_ in 1926 adds the information that the staff, in addition to Mr. Needler, was a sugar boiler and a boy named Watson. The significance of the name is unclear, but there was also a horse and cart for deliveries, so perhaps he drove this.

The sugar confectionery trade at this time was supplied by a multitude of small manufacturers, each serving an area within horse and cart radius. As we have seen, the capital requirement was very small and the technical skill came from the sugar boiler, who would be a craftsman who picked up his trade from practical experience. There might have been a thermometer, but it is more likely that he would drop a small quantity of a boiling into cold water to see if it was ready to set. The bulk ingredient would be cane sugar, with fat and milk for toffee, and a supply of flavourings. The boilings were cooled on a slab, kept cool itself by water pipes underneath, and then either broken up when set into pieces, or formed into a 'rope' and run through a hand-turned die to make the familiar sweet shape. There was no wrapping; the pack would be a cheap green glass jar, returnable when empty.

The 1880s were a very good time to start in this trade, as easy and cheap distribution of goods over a much wider area than the local one was now possible by the well organised railway system. A flourishing wholesale trade had started, and the public had realised that there was a benefit in buying products with a reliable name. I have no information about the company in these early years. It is clear that there was a steady growth and that Fred (helped by sister Lucy) worked very long hours. Not only was he building up a connection with the wholesale trade in other towns, but he started his own wholesale business in addition to manufacturing, and regular moves were needed to provide more space. The traditional list of addresses does not agree with the Hull directories, but as all were in the area to the north of Paragon Station, largely cleared when Ferensway was cut through in 1930, all must have been used at some time.

We know that he moved to 48a Brook Street in 1890 and added No.37 in 1893. The 1889 Directory shows an address in Robert Street, and a warehouse in 1892 in Mill Street. Finally much larger premises were bought for £900 at 9 and 11 Spring Street in 1898, and this is where the first written records start.

Private Life

Frederick, like any self-made business man, had little time for interests outside his work other than a life-long commitment to the Methodist Church. The non-conformist influence was very strong in the starting of many businesses; and every chocolate and confectionery business in the U.K. started from either Quaker or Methodist origins. Fred was no exception.

A new United Methodist chapel had been built on Beverley Road in 1869, at Stepney near the railway station of that name, and he was a Sunday school teacher here for many years.

The Stepney chapel connection with the family and the company was always very strong. In 1898 he married another Sunday School teacher at Stepney, Gertrude Wood, but only after he had broken off an earlier engagement and been the subject of a law suit for breach of promise.

Gertrude's father was John Wood, who came from Shepley, near Huddersfield, and worked for the North Eastern Railway. He moved to Hull to take a job in the Hull office at Paragon Station, and became the organist at Stepney Chapel.

There was another chapel influence in Fred's particular friend, Tom Burnell, a tobacco salesman. There is a very good photograph of Fred and Tom taken in the Sutcliffe studio in Whitby showing the pair very smartly dressed in blazers. Tom married Gertrude's sister Amy.

At the time of his wedding, Fred was living at 44 Chesnut Avenue, very near Queen's Road, and the Woods were at 34 Duesbery Street, off Princes Avenue.

My father, Arthur Percival, was the only child, and was born on August 18th 1900 at Grandmother Wood's house in Duesbery Street.

The earliest documents I have which directly relate to the business are a price list and a single profit and loss account for the year to April 1900. This is beautifully hand-written by the auditor, Mr. Forrester of Grimsby. A Hull firm of accountants was not used on the principle that this would avoid leaks of confidential financial information. His firm of accountants was to become Forrester, Boyd, and was still the company's auditor up to 1986.

The figures show a total turnover for manufacturing and wholesale combined of £15,000 and a profit of £781, which is about 5% on turnover. I estimate this represents about 10 tons per week, of which I would guess half as manufactured. This was not very big, but it provided a basis for growth. The photograph of the Spring Street workforce shows 10 girls and 23 men, and the wage bill was £1200.

The company was now of a size to be regarded as more than just another local sweet-maker. The price list runs to 17 pages; his own manufactured goods are 38 lines of boiled sweets, 40 of toffees, 35 of health sweets, 14 of pralines and 15 different labelled sticks of rock. In addition there are 65 boiled sweet products under the name of Spring Sweets at a cheaper price. This makes over 200 different products from the one small factory. On an estimated sale of 2500 items per week, production must have been in very small batches against firm orders received, with no attempt made to hold stocks of finished goods.

The company was an agent for Stollwerck's chocolates imported from Germany. In addition, the wholesale part of the list shows the products of Fry's, Cadbury's, Rowntree's, Craven's and Tavener's together with names no longer around today.

The Company from 1900

Growth was now faster, helped by an important decision to pioneer the use of clear glass jars to pack the sweets, which gave a much better appearance to a product which was becoming known for quality. In 1902, the first Limited Company was formed as Fred Needler Ltd. and a minute book appears. This is a most frustrating document to get a coherent story from as various entries start and are never referred to again.

The new company was incorporated on 27th October 1902; the first directors were Fred Needler, Alfred Thorpe and Joseph Cooper Wilson, with salaries of £250, £160 and £140 respectively.

The first shareholders were;

Fred Needler	5416
Alfred Thorpe	380
J.C. Wilson	150
Mrs. G.M.Needler	1
Robert Hunter	1 (described as foreman)
Jane Needler	1
Stephen Forrester	1 (auditor)

Alfred Thorpe started work in the Spring Street office in 1893 at the age of 23, but showed such promise as a salesman that he became the representative for the local area. Fred then moved him back to become the Director in charge of confectionery production, a position he held until his death in 1934, when he was succeeded by his son Clifford Thorpe. The other early director was John Burstall, a Stepney church contact, who retired about 1960, and was responsible for buying and packaging. I have been unable to find out anything about Mr. Wilson.

The continuing expansion soon meant that Spring Street was too small. In 1905 the Tower Oil Mills in Dansom Lane were under consideration as a new site; £1600 was offered to buy the premises, but this was not accepted.

A builder by the name of Christie had a yard off Sculcoates Lane at the end of Bournemouth Street with ample land attached and a part of this was therefore bought, and a purpose-built factory was started. The original buildings were a two storey office block with an entrance off the delightfully named Lotus Avenue (in reality a terrace of houses off Bournemouth Street) and a single storey factory behind. These buildings were on the edge of the Beverley and Barmston agricultural drain (See photo on page 32). There was a house in the yard which was retained; this was still there until the 1970's and was my father's office, although completely surrounded by a modern factory.

Part of the single storey factory had a first-floor addition a little later, and various other wooden buildings were added from time to time; while these have long since gone, the original brick buildings still stand (1993) and part are still in use as the outside wall of the very modern sweet-wrapping and packing plant.

There are good photographs of the new departments in the factory showing plenty of space, and a large labour force, mostly female and fashionably dressed. Between 1906 and 1914 the sales were firmly established on a national basis by means of agents, who were large wholesalers granted sole selling rights for their own areas. These were well chosen distributors, and several were still acting as sole agents until the 1960's; in particular John Esslemont in Aberdeen maintained a full coverage of all the North of Scotland until 1975. However, the agreements were open-ended, and took a good deal of disentangling in the 1950's when some of the businesses concerned had lapsed into terminal decline. I remember one with agency rights for the city of Derby which was run by two very elderly ladies, one of whom was the total office staff, and was always to be found with her knitting, while the other looked after the stock, which was all kept in very early Needler wooden boxes stacked on their sides.

The minute books record the profits from 1907, and the rate of growth was steady. Removal costs upset the 1907 figure of £733, but there is a regular increase from £2481 in 1908 to £4767 in 1914.

The increasing demand for the manufactured goods meant that the wholesale part of the operation could be run down; there is no clear date for this, but it seems to have gone by 1912.

The name of the company had been changed to Needlers Ltd. at the time of the move to Bournemouth Street in 1906. With the increase in size, there were regular issues of preference shares as bonus issues to the existing shareholders and to the longer serving employees.

Fred Needler was very much in the line of the philanthropic industrialists exemplified by the Reckitt, Rowntree and Cadbury families. He was a firm believer in the principle of profit-sharing, and a scheme was set up in 1911, which paid out an annual bonus to all employees with over two years service from a lump sum agreed by the Board. A dining room for employees was opened in 1915.

New plant was also introduced, such as the first vacuum cooking pans in England, known under the name of Eureka, which speeded up and improved the cooking process, and reduced the fuel used for cooking.

The product range in 1912 seems to have expanded to replace the wholesale trade and reaches a mind-boggling total of 576 lines. It is difficult to see how any sort of control could have been kept over factory production and stocks to cope with this, even if some of them where made outside and bought in as needed. The price list shows 74 chocolate lines, which were made in the factory by hand, using chocolate couverture from a specialist supplier. The rest of the price list can be summarised as:

49	Best Toffees
43	Caramels
224	Best Boiled Sweets
14	Cheaper toffees
34	Tins and other fancy packs
79	Pastilles and Lozenges
46	Coconut ice etc.
13	Cracknels

The Move into Chocolate Production

Fred had thought for some time that a move into chocolates was desirable. The margins on sugar confectionery have always been small because of the amount of cheap competition. Chocolate needs a much larger investment in plant and therefore needs a company of a reasonable size. In addition the scope for product branding and different packaging is very much greater. As the product list shows, he had tried out the market from 1912. An increase in profits allied to the space available on the Bournemouth Street site meant that the time had come for this major expansion. The first reference to it in the minute book is dated February 1915, when the Board agreed to look for a head of a chocolate department. Mr. Lazenby from Carsons of Bristol was appointed, and remained in that position until 1927 when he left to set up his own business in York.

The start of the chocolate factory was approved in July 1915. This is the western part of the present main 5-floor factory building (See photo on page 46). The architect was Mr. Bilson of Blanchard, Wheatley and Holdsworth, of Hull, and the expected cost "between £2000 and £3000 to be based on a 10% profit on cost" which seems a very woolly arrangement. There was in fact a problem owing to an error by Mr. Blanchard, the cost working out much higher than was originally anticipated, £200 being due to the addition of 8 feet to the length of the building to balance pillars. There was a further £400 because "the cost of the tower was deducted twice, in the first place by Mr. Bilson, and then Mr. Blanchard not knowing this, deducted it again."

The actual cost of this first part of the chocolate factory was £4188 and it was finished in August 1916. In October it was thought that this was not the right time for proceeding with any more building work in order to enlarge the factory, but Mr. Needler promised to make further enquiries, and failing this, to find out other alternatives, such as "running stuff (sic!) across to the New Building from the present Centre Room by the endless belt system or other ideas."

The chocolate factory was one of the first buildings to have a structure based entirely on reinforced concrete; there are no steel girders anywhere in the building, or in the subsequent completion. The structure has certainly been very strong, but it has left a difficult legacy in the fact no pillars or main beams can be touched, as there is a complicated network of forces carefully calculated over the whole structure, and any interference with them could cause a structural failure. As a result the building has proved very inflexible when it comes to installing large modern plant.

I have referred to the expansion of the business from 1914 to 1919. The figures are quite astonishing, and are worth examining for this period.

	Turnover	Net profit before Tax
Apl.1913-Apl.1914	£95,400	£5,100
Apl.1914-Apl.1915	112,800	10,000
Apl.1915-Dec.1915	95,300	7,000 for 9 months
1916	171,100	17,500
1917	219,000	36,200
1918	228,800	24,600
1919	446,700	101,300
1920	664,300	33,300

1920 was the absolute peak for turnover; the business then settled down to a fairly steady level up to 1926, the average profit being £50,000 on turnover of £570,000.

The reason for the transformation of the business from a small one to a medium size in such a short time is not altogether clear. The 1914 War meant that there were shortages of materials, and lack of competition and there was a bout of inflation, so that the increase in turnover is not a true reflection of the volume increase. It is clear that there were problems with materials, and part of the answer in fact lies here. In 1917, Mr. Needler had to explain that he had been receiving far too much sugar from the Commission which controlled materials, as their base figure for the company was wrong. He was called to London to sort this out, and had to agree to a stop in sugar supplies until the stock was reduced to 4 weeks' requirement. He said this would take four months, which means he had 20 weeks' stock of sugar in hand. During the period, the factory stopped Saturday working.

Another light on the raw material situation is given by a note sent out to customers in March 1918; "Kindly note we are reluctantly compelled to charge higher prices on some of our BOILED SWEETS on account of the greatly increased cost of raw materials such as Honey, which is FOUR times the price of sugar, and which helps to assist in the production.

We assume our customers would prefer paying a little more to obtain goods rather than meet the possibility of a further reduction in output."

So production was being kept up by subsitituting more expensive materials.

The other effect of course was the introduction of chocolate products in late 1916. Fred had seen a gap in the market for chocolate assortments and the growth between 1917 and 1920 was mainly due to the new products.

It is only fair to point out that many industries had found the war years made profits rise, for the same basic reasons. The Government introduced an Excess Profits Tax to restrict the actual amount a company could keep to a reasonable figure, and Needlers paid £64,000 to the Exchequer as a result.

In 1918 the idea of a pension scheme was proposed in order to use some of the profit for the benefit of the employees. The Board turned this down "as the great majority of employees were females, and even in the case of the men there were not too many who stayed for a long period". This makes odd reading today.

However they did increase the profit sharing bonus sustantially; for example, on a total wage bill of £26,500 in 1917 the bonus added was £5,000, which is 19% extra.

Family Life from 1900

In fifteen years from the start of the business, Fred had built up a good income, married and became the father of Arthur Percival (always known as Percival), their only child. They moved to 23 Marlborough Avenue shortly after 1900, only a short distance, but a move into the Avenues was a good move in the social level.

They moved again in 1917 to a large detached house at 101 Park Avenue, (Ivydene, now an old people's home) where they remained for the rest of Fred's life.

I have a domestic account book which covers most of this time; it is not very detailed and contains regular entries of "items not included", but it gives a good idea of the way of life.

The first full year in the account book is 1910, and I have summarised the figures (rounding to the nearest pound).

Household Expenses	£131
Maids Wages	13
Gas and Coal	7
Telephone	4
Rates and taxes	15
Insurance and life insurance	34
Decorating	7
Clothes	9
Gifts to wife & clothes	22
Son;clothes	4
Hymers college fees	8
Two bicycles	6
Turton, Dentist	12
Allowance to mother	71
Charitable gifts	76
Golf	5
Holiday;Easter	3
Keswick	8
Cowley; Boots	1
Browns; Books	1
Gough & Davy; Music	2
Bladons; Furniture	21
Picture	2
Curtains	2
Plumber	2
Hobson; China	2
Doctor Fraser	2
Doctor Cumming	3
Doctor Martin	1
Lit & Phil subsciption	1
Misc. cash	55
Unidentified	37
Year's total	567
Income	693 Surplus £126

The figures look impossibly low by 1993 standards; it is not easy to convert to our current levels, as wage rates have altered so much and this has a very different effect on various items; however a rough factor of 20 can be applied, which gives by 1993 standards an income £13,800, with no tax and rates of only £300. There was a maid who lived in, and the wages allowed for this so she got 5 shillings (25p) a week. The only figure that looks high by present day standards is that for Mr. Turton, the dentist, who comes in regularly at between £12 and £20, while the doctor's fees only come to £6. Fred always paid at least 10% of his income to charities, which included the Stepney Chapel, and this is carefully worked out in his cash book, where he takes his annual income divided by 10 and lists all his gifts to make sure that they reach the right figure. He was by now maintaining his mother, who was living at 98 de Grey Street, and died in 1917 at the age of 83. There is some mystery attatched to Fred's brother Henry. He was working as a salesman for the company up to about 1910, and appears to have been very useful, from the cash figures he paid in, which are in an old day book. He never married, and became an alcoholic. How bad this was, I cannot judge, as the family were good Methodist non-drinkers, and were always very secretive about Henry; he was certainly being supported financially by Fred after 1910. In October 1913 his cash book lists a train fare to Gloucester for Henry with an additional entry for a doctor's certificate, so it appears that he was sent to some institution there. He died in 1915 in another home in Aylesbury at the age of 44 and is buried with his mother in the Spring Bank cemetery.

There really is very little other evidence about Fred's family life; I get a picture of a man very fully occupied with his growing business and dedicated to the work of Stepney Chapel. He was always a supporter of the Liberal party, and used to produce specially printed toffee tins for the local candidates to give away at election times, a practice which would not be allowed now. He used to cycle to work, and had taken up golf. He was never spoilt by his increasing affluence, giving freely to charities and family members in need, helping his good friend Tom Burnell financially, and establishing profit-sharing, canteen facilities and welfare provisions for his factory workers long before such things became usual.

His son Percival contracted polio in the 1905 epidemic; this left him with a weak left leg, and he had a pronounced limp for the rest of his life. The family consulted many doctors, and finished up with a London consultant, but the damage had been done and it was too late to find a cure.

It is sad that only two letters written by Fred have survived. I reproduce one of these; it was written to his son Percival who was away on holiday in August 1922.

Dear Percival,
        By the time this reaches you it will be your birthday. I was in town today thinking of what I could get for you, but finding nothing I decided to celebrate it by buying myself a pipe and mother a fur coat. I don't know how you will benefit by this unless your own pipe smokes sweeter, knowing I have got a new one.

However, I wish you many happy returns of the day; you are wiser I am sure than when you were twenty-one, but there is a lot to know yet and you are going well in the way of getting to know.

We are quieter here for your absence. This can be read two ways, but it is agreeable to me to have a fellow to discuss things with - Lord Northcliffe - the break-up of the conference - Lloyd George's memoirs and his getting £90,000 for them; good gracious, what are one's public men coming to.

We are kept busy with plenty of work, and I have got a gardener-chaffeur coming on Monday....

Your affectionate Father.

The Completion of the Chocolate Factory

As soon as the war finished, it became possible to finish the chocolate factory. The 5-floor building which already existed was about a third of the total planned. For some reason the architects were changed to Jacobs and Snowden, and they suggested a cost of £14,500, which Mr. Needler had checked out as 1½ times the original cost because of the increase in size, and a factor of 2 for inflation. There must have been something very wrong about this idea, because it was dropped, and an architect, one Mr. Rickartson, was appointed as an employee. By January 1920 it had been decided to build in two phases, and a two-storey L-shaped block was approved, with foundations to allow for the subsequent addition of the other floors. The cost of this new scheme was quoted as £28,450 for the first part, which seems to show the costs for the earlier plan were not right. It was built by a builder called J.H.Fenwick, and was ready by September 1919 at a final cost of £50,168 and £5984 for a new boiler house and chimney. This is nearly twice the contract figure, and there is a detailed list of payments showing how this total is arrived at, but no comment anywhere about this.

The 1921 drawing shows the factory at this stage (See photo on page 46), but the final completion to five floors throughout was delayed until 1925. The cost of this was only £25,000, so much of the extra must have gone on foundations and services in 1920.

The building still stands today (1993), but the very large modern plant has all gone into a new building to the south on what used to be Bournemouth Street, the houses having been demolished in 1972.

The 1920's

The company went into the post-war years as a much bigger concern than in 1914. There are no figures of volumes but based on an average turnover of £570,000 per year, I estimate an annual output of 650 tons of chocolate and 1500 tons of sweets. The peak level of employment in the autumn when Christmas boxes were being made was 1700 employees, the majority being female, and many engaged on a seasonal basis for the Christmas and Easter trade. The number fell to about 1000 in the summer months. To put this into perspective, the company had become one of the largest employers in the city of Hull in a very short period of time, and had a very high local reputation. We have to remember that the chocolate and confectionery trade is a very big one in the U.K., and I estimate a national production of 300,000 tons, so the Needler figure of 2150 must have been less than 1% of the market. This is a very awkward size, as the company had all the standard business problems of building up a management to cope with the internal growth, while being unable to grow into a size to be a truly national company. In fact, this problem was never solved. The sales force was built up to about 30, and the advertising budget for chocolate assortments was increased to about 8% of turnover.

The name of Needler as a maker of chocolate assortments became quite well known, but a large proportion of this trade came at Christmas with the attendant problems of building up stocks, and a peak of profits at the end of the year.

The Products

The 1929 price list does show a fall in the number of lines on offer compared with 1912, but it is still bewildering in its size. Apart from Christmas boxes and Easter eggs there are chocolate assortments, each in 4-6 different packs;

6/- per lb	(30p)	Minaret.
		Kiro.
5/6	(27p)	Albany.
5/-	(25p)	Melsa.
4/-	(20p)	Lido.
		Wilberforce.
		Elite.
		Assorted Chocolate Nuts.
		Carlton.
		Crown Derby.
		Eldora.
		County.

There are many chocolate bars at 2d for 2oz (about 1p) and also bars in larger sizes.
There are;   40   toffee covered lines.
                    140   boiled sweets.
                    21   pastilles.
Plus 4 pages of fancy packs such as tins.

The real weakness is that there are no obvious brand leaders by this stage, and there was no real growth after 1920.

Mr. Needler's concern over the situation is shown by several comments of his at company annual meetings; for example, in 1922 "the chocolate trade is rather a puzzle; we have invested over £90,000 in this, and it is a matter of concern that we have such a small output.". At another place he refers to the production facility being only half used.

In 1925 he was saying "Wages have increased by £8000 due to the fact that the wage structure increased with age (i.e. ages 15 to 21 had a built-in increase at each birthday); thus we have the same staff as the year before, but the wage bill goes up. There is also heavy overtime for the Christmas trade."

The problem of the girls' wage rate kept on coming up, due to the fact that girls taken on when they left school did not leave. The job was clean and in comfortable surroundings, and by the late 1920's 80% of the employees were on full adult rates. As was the general rule at that time, however, any girl getting married had to leave, but did receive a wedding present, size dependant on length of service.

There was a long service association for girls over 15 years service and men over 20 years service and this comprised the bulk of the employees. The factory had become a show-piece; there were welfare facilities for employees ahead of their time; the pension scheme for men started in 1922; there were sports teams for football, netball, cricket, and swimming, and land had been bought off Clough Road to make a cricket and football ground.

Fred Needler was a good friend of Tom Ferens of Reckitts, a fellow Methodist, and was approached by him at the time he was founding the University College, later to become Hull University. As a result Fred personally bought a house in Cottingham and donated it to the University as a residential hall, still known as Needler Hall. He never lived there, but lived in Park Avenue to the end of his life.

Much money had been spent on the factory. A box-making and printing plant had been set up under Mr. Batten so that boxes could be made as needed for packing. All packing areas were fully air-conditioned in 1927, which was a pioneering advance enabling packing to continue in all weathers without sweets becoming sticky, or chocolates becoming soft.

There were many visits to the factory, and parties were encouraged from customers to organise a day out to visit the factory. The high point was a visit from Edward, Prince of Wales in 1926 when he was in Hull for a day, and also went to Reckitt's.

Transport of Goods to Customers

Until 1918, all goods were either delivered locally by horse-drawn van, or sent in wooden boxes by rail. This was clearly not suitable for increased volumes, and a fleet of delivery vans was built up, working from Hull, and from rail-served depots in London (at Hornsey goods yard), Manchester and Nottingham. There was also a depot in Grimsby which was served by a daily container shipped direct from Hull. This was a daily service which ran from a wharf off High Street, and was still running in the 1950's.

The vehicle fleet totalled 40 vans by 1927; the livery settled down to the well-known chocolate brown, and was regarded as good advertising, so considerable pride was taken in the appearance. The vehicles were fitted internally with wooden shelves, and were individually coach-built by the Hull firm of Barnabys.

The vans in the 1920's were either Thorneycroft or Maudsley, with acetylene lamps and solid rubber tyres. The drivers had to ensure that fully loaded vans were not parked too long in one position, as the tyres would develop flat spots, and would then be very rough-riding. The photographs show that the speed limit on all vehicles was 20 mph, and only raised to 30 mph in 1930.

The vehicle fleet was maintained until 1965, when there were over 50 vans and drivers, with a mate each to help with the deliveries. The vans still had shelves inside, and were loaded by a gang of three, who threw the boxes and jars to one another, the last one putting them on the shelves. The rail-served depots were replaced by road containers after 1950, as British Rail increased the use of hump-shunting, and it was not possible to protect the jars against breakage. A really bad shunt would break every jar in the container.

The vans went as distribution changed into 40-foot containers travelling overnight to contract distribution services. In the 1920's and 30's, there were a number of show vans, which had a full display of products inside, and some items in windows outside as well; these were driven by salesmen, who drove them to the customers' premises so the large range of chocolates could be seen. These vans were all requisitioned by the Army in 1939, but it was not clear what use they were put to; they were never seen again.

The Depression

After 1926, the profits started to fall, and as money became tight, the turnover also dropped. Mr. Needler was aware of coming problems allied to the lack of growth, and in 1926 went to look at production methods in the USA, taking his son Percival and Clifford Thorpe with him.

They visited a number of large factories, and they noted particularly:

1. Much higher co-operation between employers, employees and unions in accepting change.
2. US hours 50 per week against 46 in UK.
3. Wages. Skilled man in UK 75 to 85 shillings per week (£3.75 to £4.25), In US 35 dollars - £7 per week. Girls in UK 20 to 30 shillings (£1 to £1.50), In US £2.50 to £2.75

As a result of the higher wages, the Americans had large factories, with very much more mechanisation, although the group were not impressed by the actual quality of the products. They concluded that a higher volume of production was needed in Hull. While this was undoubtedly correct, nowhere in the notes is there any attempt to have a fundamental look at increasing the volume of sales.

While I believe Fred Needler would have dealt with this, unfortunately by 1927 at the age of 62 he started to show signs of illness, and had to take a lighter workload, just as the effects of the trade depression were showing.

Mr. Lazenby, who had been running the chocolate factory, left to set up his own business in York.

Fred's son, Percival was appointed Vice-Chairman responsible for exports, sales policy and advertising, and the Board had to settle down to keeping the company afloat. This was achieved, but the worst year 1931 showed a turnover of only £328,000, down to 40% of the early 1920's average. The profit was just over break-even at £5,100.

By this time, Fred was an invalid with Parkinson's disease, and he died on 30 September 1932, at the age of 67.

His passing was noted with long articles in both local and regional newspapers; I cannot do better than quote from some remarks of a well-known Methodist Minister, Rev. Albert Bluck, who said:

"He was a faithful friend and a splendid type of Christian gentleman... success and honours had not injured his character... I cannot describe the singular charm of his winsome character. I never knew him to fail in honour or in kindness, or in good sense, or in humour."

Needlers Musical Society

One of the more unusual company activities was the mixed-voice choir which was founded in 1925 and was made up almost entirely from employees, with some husbands and wives included. Originally conducted by Richard Sales, Mr. J.W. Rossington took over in the 1930's. With about 50 members, the choir became well-known on the Music Festival competition circuit, and won many prizes. It broadcast on the BBC in 1935, and presented concerts in Hull, often with quite adventurous programmes, such as a Delius concert conducted by Eric Fenby, who had been the composer's amanuensis when he became paralysed. The choir was finally disbanded in 1947 when the employee support for this type of activity had changed after the war. I have included a photograph of the choir in 1938, as this has a full list of names.

The musical society in 1938.
Back row; H.A. Goodison, H. Latus, G. Hoe S. Ritchie, A.H. Ransome, A.Leadbeater, R.Cook, S.Spedding, H.Hairsine, T.Jefferson.
Third row; J.A. Shaw, H.F. Dick, E.G. Ashurst, Mrs. D. Harland, Miss M. Borrill, Miss L. Robinson, Miss W. Mitchell, Miss P. Wright, Miss E. Horsfield, Mrs. C. Brown, T. Cooper, A. Linskill, A. Clayton.
Second Row; Miss J. Cook, Mrs. J. Swainson, Mrs. P. McCormish, Miss G.M. Lowday, Miss V. Waterland, Miss E. Stothard, Mrs. D. Smith, Mrs. J. Foley, Mrs. F. Barber, Miss E. Mitchell, Miss M. Watson, Mrs. F. White, Miss K. Clark, Miss A. Gray.
Front Row; Miss E. Tozer, Miss M. Werner, Mrs. R.A. Sales, Mrs. S. Ritchie, Mr. R.A. Sales, Mr. J.W. Rossington,(Conductor), Mrs. F. Needler (President) Mr. J.H. Foley, Mr. F.N. Wood, Mrs. N. Hairsine, Miss C. Steeley, Miss B. McClaren, Miss F. Marshall.

The Business After Fred Needler's Death

Fred's son Percival took over as Managing Director in 1932. For the record, the senior management was:

A. Thorpe, Production Director.
Fred Twell, Sales Director.
J.T.Burstall, Packaging Director.

SECRETARY   A. Wood
MANAGERS   Mr. Grassam, Accounts and statistics,
            Mr. Hattan, Yard and transport.
            Mr. Holyman, Advertising.
            Mr. Harry Gray, Assistant to Mr. Wood.
            Mr. Evans, Engineer (Followed by Mr. Hartley).
            Mr. Marritt, Export.
            Mr. A.P. Smith, Centre department.
            Mr. Gowland, Chief chemist.
            Mr. W. Rawson, General office.
            Miss Livingstone, Personnel.

Mr. C.P. Thorpe was assistant to his father in production, and took over from him after Alfred Thorpe died in 1934.

During the early 1920's it had been decided to start to wrap some caramels and a few boiled sweets individually. As there was no machinery available to do this, it meant hand wrapping each sweet, a method which seems impossible today, and must have been very tedious. Wrapping machines were not introduced until 1928, but soon all sweets were being wrapped by Needlers, although there were still plenty of cheap unwrapped products on the market. All sweet sales were weighed out in the shop from the glass jar in quarter pound units; the pre-pack bag as we now know it only appeared in the 1950's.

Economic conditions remained poor, and the main development was in cheaper chocolate assortments under the names of Oxford & Cambridge, and the introduction of new plant to make 2oz. chocolate bars, selling at 2d. (less than 1p), under a new brand name, Kreema. The advertising of chocolates was maintained and a satisfactory increase in profits was achieved in 1934.

This recovery did not last; the sales of chocolate fell again due to lack of money, and were replaced by increasing sales of boiled sweets, which were much cheaper, but carried less profit.

Percival was not the entrepreneurial type of business man as his father was, and found the running of the company a considerable strain.. He was able to keep a very good control over everything with the help of a capable management team, but was unable to change the overall pattern of the business, which remained as about half chocolate and half sugar confectionery and always stayed profitable.

There was one important development in 1938. Clifford Thorpe and Mr. Gowland, the chemist, found a way of depositing boiled sugars in a sweet-sized mould. All sweets and toffees were still made by the old process of forming the cooked batch into a rope and running this between the dies. While this was now done on modern plant, the product had to be made in small batches, and fruit drops and similar lines were inevitably cloudy, due to the trapped air.

If the traditional boiling was put into a mould, it crystallised when cold into an unusable product. By the application of simple chemistry a method of making a clear deposited fruit drop was discovered, and home-made plant installed to make this. It was introduced under the name of Glace Fruit Drop, but was just one of the many lines on the product list.

It was in the post-war days that this Glace Fruit Drop had the market to itself until 1965, and transformed the balance of the business to basically a sugar confectionery manufacturer.

The Company from 1940

A brief summary.

From 1941 until February 1953 sweets were rationed to the public, and the supply of materials was very tightly controlled. Nothing changed from the 1939 pattern of trade, although the absence of competition meant that profits were good.

At the end of rationing, the consumption of sweets and chocolate went up and stayed at a figure of half a pound of sweets and chocolates per person per week. The effect on Needlers was that the demand for Glace Fruit Drops went far above production capacity and it was not until 1957 when another three home-made plants had been put into service that the supply caught up. As the demand for other sugar confectionery made by the company had stayed buoyant, and chocolate sales were increasingly going to the Cadbury/Rowntree/Mars groups, the company started to find itself as a predominantly sugar confectionery maker.

There was a very large increase in sales value and profits, and in 1958 the company became a public company with a quotation on the London Stock Exchange, although the Needler family retained a controlling holding.

It was astonishing that the process for making deposited sweets was not discovered by other companies until 1965, when plant appeared on the market. The end of the uniqueness of the product led to poorer profits from 1966. In 1970 Percival Needler and Clifford Thorpe both retired at the age of 70 and I took over as Managing Director.

We had accumulated a considerable cash balance, and the business of Batger, based in London was acquired, and moved to Hull. This added a valuable toffee business under the brand of Jersey Toffee and contracts with the multiple grocers such as Sainsbury. Needler sales had been entirely in the glass jars, and we now moved into the growing pre-packed film bag trade.

A new management team enabled us to install a better financial control system, which showed that the remaining small chocolate trade was losing money. The results stayed poor, and in 1976 there was a loss of over half a million pounds. As a result, chocolate production was ended, and the labour employed reduced by half to 400; the financial result of concentration on sugar confectionery was immediately obvious, and a record profit was made in 1977. A major investment programme was started in large continuous plant fot the manufacture of deposited sweets and toffees, and new lines introduced with soft centres under the name of Sensations.

Major export markets were established for the first time in the early 1980's, particularly in the Middle East and USA.

In 1986 an offer to buy the business was accepted from Hillsdown Holdings, a large meat company expanding at that time into other areas. In 1987 I retired from the company and Brian Whittle took over as Managing Director. The expected development by Hillsdown into a large confectionery group did not happen after the purchase of Bluebird Toffee proved to be a mistake. Needlers were sold by Hillsdown to NORA SA, the largest food group in Norway, who have continued to develop the business in Hull, which remains on the same Sculcoates Lane site.

Appendix 1

Table of turnover and profit from 1909

Year (May-Apl.)	Turnover £'000	Profit before tax £'000	
1909	69	2.9	
1910	80	3.6	
1911	83	3.8	
1912	93	4.0	
1913	95	4.8	
1914	113	10.0	
1915	95	6.2	8 months only
Jan-Dec.			
1916	171	17.5	
1917	219	36.2	
1918	229	24.6	
1919	447	101.3	
1920	664	33.3	
1921	522	32.8	
1922	512	53.5	
1923	573	63.2	
1924	564	49.3	
1925	590	58.9	
1926	570	50.0	
1927	557	34.9	
1928	521	32.1	
1929	478	26.4	
1930	382	15.8	
1931	328	5.1	
1932	331	6.6	
1933	328	12.7	
1934	406	51.6	
1935	425	42.6	
1936	465	41.0	
1937	N/A	24.2	
1938	469	24.2	
1939	532	47.1	

Appendix 2

LONG SERVICE EMPLOYEES: a list of the earliest names.

Women. Over 12 years service.

Year of starting	Names Miss;	Married name, if known.
1903	M. Pratt	
	M. Houlden	
1905	I. Thomson	
	C. Steeley	
1906	A. Smith	
	E. Bennison	
1907	V. Pickering	
1908	M. Taylor	
	J. Waldron	Cox
	E. Ellis	
1909	N. Beecher	
	E. Pye	
	G. Davis	Metcalfe
	E. Whiting	Pitts
	D. Armstrong	Fearnside
1910	L. Cuthbert	Cornwell
	A. Kelwick	
	L. Bricklebank	Wilburne
1911	M. Donaldson	Taylor
	G. Davis	Metcalfe
	M. Johnson	Wiles
	A. Swinn	Jackson
	D. Wilkinson	
	K. Wright	Ostler
	E.O. Cockerill	Murray
	D.L. Wilmore	
	F. Piercy	

Men. Over 20 years service. (excluding directors)

1889	C. Yeomans
1890	Alf Nicholls
1892	G. Langdale
	F.W. Thorpe
	G.W. Atkinson
1896	A. Gray
1899	E. Miller
1902	S. Ross
	T.H. Plowright
	T.W. Douglas
1903	R. Wiles
	H. Gray
1904	Tom Hunter
	Frank Mellis
1905	A.P. Smith

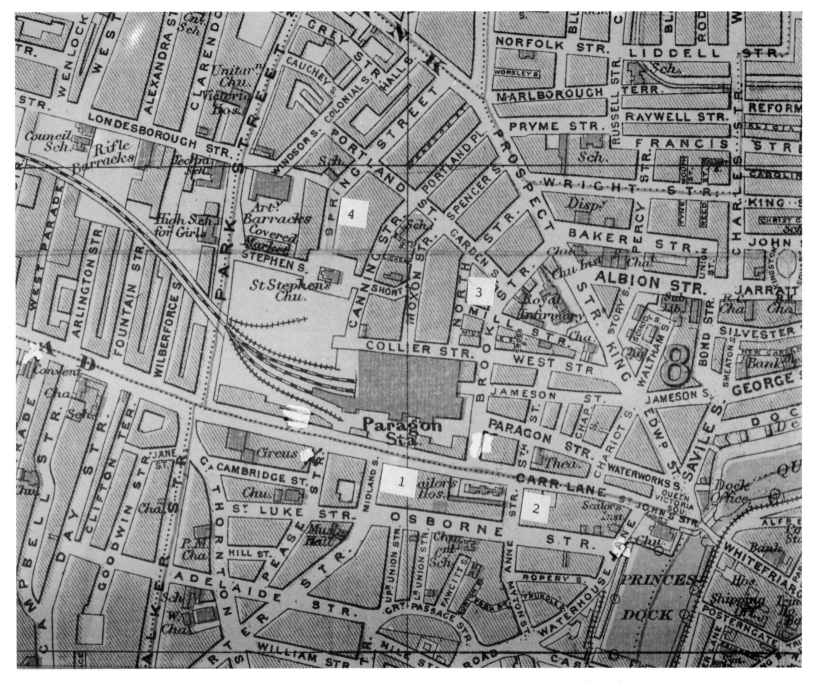

*Map of the area around Paragon Station before Ferensway was cut through,
showing approximate positions of the early premises.
1. Mr. Buckton's factory.   2. Anne Street.
3. Brook Street.   4. Spring Street.*

25

A drawing, stated to be the original Anne Street premises. This was used in 1936 for a booklet on the first 50 years, so it must be assumed to be correct. I do not know the source of the drawing, and the building looks too large for a business employing only 3 people.

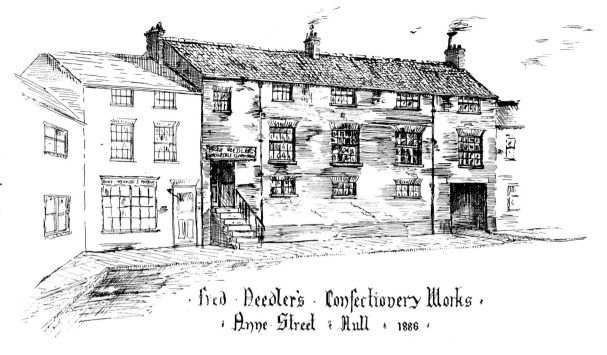

Fred · Needler's · Confectionery Works ·
· Anne · Street · Hull · 1886 ·

The factory at 48a Brook Street, 1890, and the show room at 37 Brook Street in 1894. Again the drawings are anonymous.

FRED · NEEDLER'S CONFECTIONERY WORK
BROOK STREET HULL 1890

THE STOCK & SHOW ROOM
BROOK M. 1894

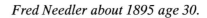
Fred Needler about 1895 age 30.

Tom Burnell (on the left) with Fred Needler.
Taken in the Sutcliffe studios in Whitby about 1890.

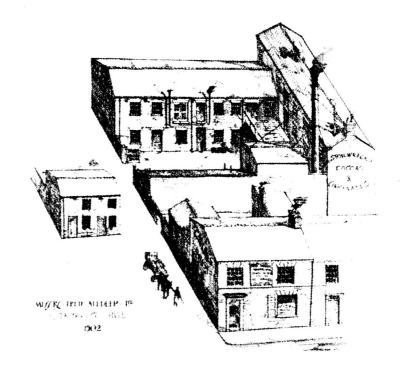

An artist's impression of the Spring Street factory dated 1902. It was in use from 1896 to 1906.

The earliest photograph of the business, showing Spring Street employees about 1900. Alfred Thorpe standing on far left.

FRED NEEDLER'S WEDDING PHOTOGRAPH. 7th September 1898.
Back Row; J.J. Clifton, Albert Buffey, Harry Needler, Frank Wood.
MIddle Row; Mrs. Hargreaves, Mr. Hargreaves, Lucy Needler, Jane Needler, Mrs. Wood, John Wood, Aunt Ramsden, Aunt Emma, Vicar,
Aunt Lindley.
Seated; Selina Needler, Flora Wood, Bride & Bridegroom, Amy Wood, Tom Burnell, Arthur Wood.
Notes; Mr. Clifton married Selina, Alburt Buffey married Lucy.
Mrs. Hargreaves was Tom Burnell's sister.
The bride's brothers and sisters were Amy. Flora, Frank and Arthur Wood.
The various Aunts were Wood relations.

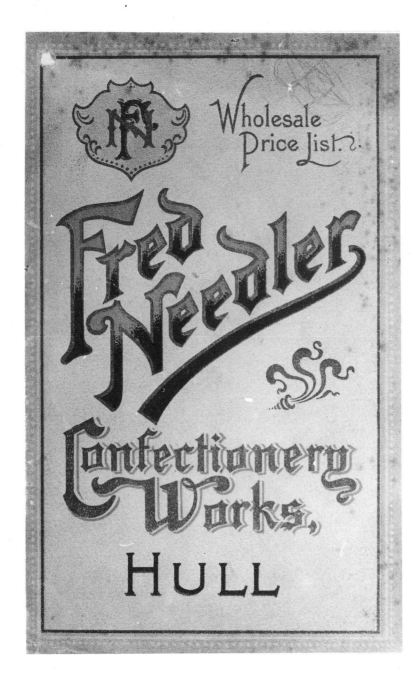

Inside cover of 1899 price list.

Cover of price list 1899.

FRED NEEDLER,

Works—9 & 11, SPRING STREET, HULL.
Office—11, SPRING STREET, HULL.

Branch Establishment—

1, SOUTH PARADE, HILDERTHORPE,
BRIDLINGTON QUAY.

Agent for Fry's, Cadbury's, Rowntree's, Stollwerck's, Allen's,
Clarke, Nickolls & Coombe's Chocolates ; and Barratt & Co.'s,
Faulder's, Terry's, Craven's and other makers of First-class
Confectionery ; Dealer in Show Glasses, Glass Dishes,
Scales, and Shop Fittings, etc.

TERMS.
• • •

Carriage Paid on **25/-** worth of Goods and upwards, less 2½ per
cent. for cash on journey.

EMPTIES.—These should be returned as soon as possible, **Carriage
Paid,** and advised in detail. We allow in full for all cases, bottles,
&c., sent out by us, when received in good condition, but cannot
allow for others. We advise receipt of all empties on arrival, and
customers may then deduct the amount for which they have received
Credit Notes.

BREAKAGES.—When receiving Goods please sign for them **"not
examined,"** and if there are any breakages advise the Railway
Company *at once.* This allows us to make a claim on the carriers
in case of damage or shortage, or carriers will not recognise claim.

Cash to accompany Order. Credit Account opened by special arrangement.

Prices are subject to market fluctuations.

*Jars of FRENCH ALMOND ROCK and WALNUT TOFFEE
about 1905.
The price is 3½ pence (1½ p) per quarter.
The sweets are in stick form, to be broken in the shop.*

*Jars of sweets about 1905, when the name FRED NEEDLER
was changed to NEEDLERS.
The price is 2oz. for one penny, which is a quarter pound for
under 1p in decimal coinage.
KHAKI MIXTURE is a name used during the Boer War;
MRS. SQUEERS COUGH DROPS seems a curious choice, as it
must refer to the terrible owners of Dotheboys Hall in Dickens'
Nicholas Nickleby.*

31

NEEDLER LTD CONFECTIONERY WORKS
SCULCOATES, HULL.

This shows the Sculcoates Lane factory as it was built in 1906. The Beverley and Barmston agricultural drain is in the left foreground. The main building is the office, with the factory behind. In the distance is the Hull and Barnsley railway which ran on the north boundary of the site. Artistic licence has made the site look about twice as large as it was.

Three pictures taken from postcards in 1906, just after the move to Sculcoates Lane. This one shows a group of employees.
The uniforms are smart, mostly with bow ties. The front row have heavy overalls for boiled sweet making; the polka dot dresses would be for the packing areas.

A CORNER IN OUR JUBE MAKING ROOM.

Described as "Jube making"; ju-jubes was the name for jellies or pastilles, which are being hand-deposited into starch trays by the man on the left.

Basic boiled sweet production; the open cooking pans are out of sight on the right.

Fred, Gertie and Percival at Marlborough Avenue in 1907.

This batch of photgraphs were taken for publicity purposes about 1910.
This shows the boiling room, with Eureka vacuum pans at the back on the right. The cold slabs are next to them, then the powered dies,
run from the overhead belts. The finished sweets lie on the tables in the foreground.
Note the large gas lights.
The source of power for the overhead drives is unknown to me, but must have been some type of steam engine.

36

No. 2 boiling room. The cooked sugars have been formed into a rope and are about to go through the hand-turned die to be formed into sweets. The front table is making humbugs, with stripes.
Note the primitive gas lighting; this department had not yet been up-dated with better lighting or power drives.

Toffee department. The cooking pans are out of sight on the right. The production is of a nougat, formed into slabs and cut on the circular cutters, one of which is seen in the middle of the picture. The overhead power drives are to the rollers which levelled the cooked mass into slabs.

Part of the pan room, about 1910.
This is one process that can still be seen today in smaller factories. The revolving pans coat almonds and other centres in sugar.

Starch room. Gums, jellies and pastilles were made here, by depositing the cooked mixture into trays of starch, using the hand pourer which is held by the girl in the middle. The sweets were allowed to dry and harden, and then sieved out in the power-driven machine at the back. The starch was re-used. The same basic process is still used, but is now highly mechanised.
A.P. Smith was the manager of this department until the 1940's, when Tom Blanchard (on the far left) took over.

Packing department, about 1910.
As the glass jars were sent by rail, they were well packed in wooden cases with straw, each case containing one customer's order.

Caramel wrapping, about 1910.
These sweets which needed protection from going sticky, were wrapped by hand.
There are about 50 girls at the back to do this,
and another 20 at the front to weigh and pack into jars or boxes.

Jar packing, about 1910.
The sweets have come in from production in the metal bins with lids, seen front left.
They are weighed and hand-packed into the jars which are labelled (front right) and carried into the racks at the back.
Many girls were employed here; there are 40 on this picture.

1910. Stock-room for boxed goods.
Some of the boxes are marked "Stollwerck", so this store includes goods bought
in for re-sale, as well as Hull manufacture of caramels etc.
The pipes are for heating; there is a radiator behind the girl on the right.

A stand at a trade show before 1914. This shows the enormous range of boiled sweets; there are about 120 different items on show and four different types of glass jar, all with glass stoppers.

This is the only photograph I know of the shop in King Edward Street, Hull.
It was opened in 1910 to be a showplace for the full range of products; between the Wars there was often a display of hand-piping of chocolates, and Easter Eggs were available to order with individual names on in chocolate. The shop was destroyed in the 1941 air-raids and not re-opened.

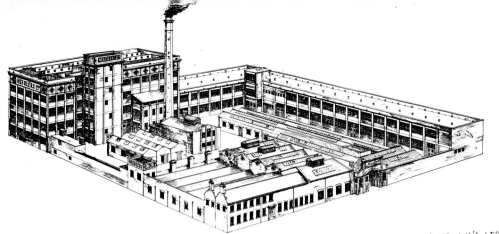

Line drawing of the factory in 1921.
The Bournemouth Street entrance is middle of the front, with the office block to the left.
The five-floor chocolate building is behind the chimney; the rest of the main block is only 2 floors, to be completed by 1925 to the full five-floor height.

The only photograph of the chocolate factory as originally built in 1916. The rest of the 5 floor building was added in 1926.

The factory in 1921, from the North.
The new two-floor L-shaped extension can be seen, with the 1916 five floor block on the right.
The Hull and Barnsley railway line in the foreground, and the new electricity power station to the right.
The Beverley & Barmston agricultural drain runs between the two factories.

The factory after 1927.
The main 5-floor block is finished; the older factory is in front to the left. Bournemouth Street and houses in the foreground.
Extreme left is the Beverley and Barmston agricultural drain, and the Hull & Barnsley railway line is immediately behind the factory.
The Sports field with the new cricket pavilion is on the other side of the railway.
Clough Road is at the top.

46

*Jars of medicated sweets in the early 1920's.
Price is 7 pence (3p) per quarter.
SAFETY FIRST COUGH TABLETS
"Prevention is better than cure"; LINSEED,
LICORICE and CHLORODYNE
LOZENGES.*

*BUTTERED BRAZILS, about 1920.
8 pence (3¹/2p) per quarter, unwrapped, which was an
expensive product. They were hand-dipped in toffee, a process
which remained until about 1960.
Note the special lid, which contains a pad to keep
the product dry.*

Jars of BUTTERMINTS & MALTONA TOFFEE. These are sixpence (2¹/2p) per quarter, and date from about 1920. They are still unwrapped

BRONCHIAL PASTILLES, late 1920's, in jars and a hand made roll pack. This was a very popular line until the 1960's, when its sales had to stop as the product contained a fair amount of chloroform, which became a banned product for food use. They were usually known as BRONX or BRONICALS.

A shop window display, about 1920.
This form of advertising was very common, but died out after 1940.
Professional window dressers were used, who toured an area on a free-lance basis for various manufacturers.

Some of the chocolate boxes about 1925. The brand names of County and Melsa were to be used for many years.

A very early photograph of display jars, specially packed for shop windows.

This is part of a well-known postcard of Spring Bank, looking away from the city centre in 1905.
The horse-drawn van was used for local deliveries, and the driver is a Mr. Douglas, whose son Charles was later the company's transport manager.
The Yorkshire Post poster outside Mr. Coults newsagents reads "Japan's advance in Manchuria", referring to the Russo-Japanese war of 1904/05. The back of the van has the company's National telephone number, which was 90X.

AT 1917, a Belsize 10-12 HP, 1 ton van with two salesmen. The van was registered in 1914, and I think the pictures date from the same year.
Note the turn-out of the men with bowler hats and waistcoates with watch chains.

*The same van outside
L. Bridgewater's
Temperance Bar.
I do not know where this is, but
the rendered buildings with
stone window copings look
Scottish.*

*Maudsley Lorry AT 6291
outside the factory entrance
with export orders for
South America.
The lorry was one of two
registered in 1922.*

COLOUR PLATES

These are all taken from various general and Christmas catalogues produced each year for the trade.
The pictures were produced by black and white photography, and each one was then coloured by hand, using water colours;
a highly skilled job.
The coloured pictures were then turned into three-colour separations for printing,
which was done in the company's own printing plant.

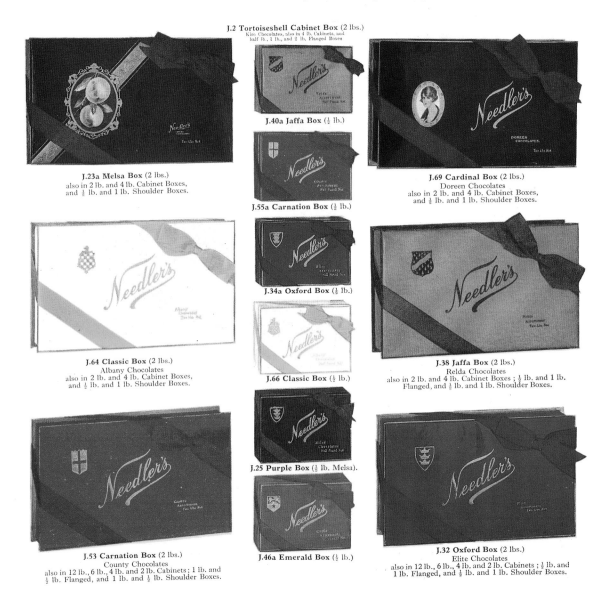

J.2 Tortoiseshell Cabinet Box (2 lbs.)
Kiro Chocolates, also in 4 lb. Cabinets, and
half lb., 1 lb., and 2 lb. Flanged Boxes

J.40a Jaffa Box (½ lb.)

J.23a Melsa Box (2 lbs.)
also in 2 lb. and 4 lb. Cabinet Boxes,
and ½ lb. and 1 lb. Shoulder Boxes.

J.55a Carnation Box (½ lb.)

J.69 Cardinal Box (2 lbs.)
Doreen Chocolates
also in 2 lb. and 4 lb. Cabinet Boxes,
and ½ lb. and 1 lb. Shoulder Boxes.

J.64 Classic Box (2 lbs.)
Albany Chocolates
also in 2 lb. and 4 lb. Cabinet Boxes,
and ½ lb. and 1 lb. Shoulder Boxes.

J.34a Oxford Box (½ lb.)

J.66 Classic Box (½ lb.)

J.38 Jaffa Box (2 lbs.)
Relda Chocolates
also in 2 lb. and 4 lb. Cabinet Boxes ; ½ lb. and 1 lb.
Flanged, and ½ lb. and 1 lb. Shoulder Boxes.

J.25 Purple Box (½ lb. Melsa).

J.53 Carnation Box (2 lbs.)
County Chocolates
also in 12 lb., 6 lb., 4 lb. and 2 lb. Cabinets ; 1 lb. and
½ lb. Flanged, and 1 lb. and ½ lb. Shoulder Boxes.

J.46a Emerald Box (½ lb.)

J.32 Oxford Box (2 lbs.)
Elite Chocolates
also in 12 lb., 6 lb., 4 lb. and 2 lb. Cabinets ; ½ lb. and
1 lb. Flanged, and ½ lb. and 1 lb. Shoulder Boxes.

FROM THE 1926 CATALOGUE.
12 of the range of over 100 different boxes of chocolates.

PRINCE OF WALES SELECTION.
A beautiful Assortment of Boiled Sweets. One of our standard and most popular lines.

This Hexagonal Container will be very useful to the Housewife.

2-LB. NETT 5/- EACH.

CHOCOLATE BON BONS.
Something new. A crisp casing with Assorted Chocolate Centres.

NIAGARA MINTS.
Clear as crystal and an excellent aid to digestion.

ROYAL BUTTER MINTS.
Delicious Butter Mint with soft eating centre.

1-lb. tin BUTTERED BRAZILS
The ever popular Buttered Brazils in air-tight tin **2/9**

VANITY BOX.
Dainty fluted ribboned diamond shaped casket in blue, containing 1-lb. nett County Chocolates de Luxe. **6/-**

FROM THE 1926 CATALOGUE.
Note that the sweets are still unwrapped, except for the Bon Bons,
which were wrapped individually by hand.

Maudsley 4 ³/₄ ton van AT 7254 registered January 1923 in Bournemouth Street, with 2 other vehicles.

Maudsley 4 ³/₄ ton van in Paragon Square, Hammonds store to the left behind, Cenotaph not yet erected. Probably 1923.

Ford AT 5624, new in 1920, decorated for a prize.

Piccadilly Selection
(in 4 lb. Dri-Dome Jars.)

Colonial Fruit Bon-Bons
(in attractive Transparent
Tubes, packed in Boxes
containing ½ Doz. Tubes.)

Colonial Fruit Bon-Bons
(in attractive Transparent
Tubes, packed in Boxes
containing ½ Doz. Tubes.)

Prince of Wales Selection
(in 4 lb. Dri-Dome Jars.)

**Mixed Fruit
Pastilles**
(in ¼ lb. and
½ lb. Cartons.)

**Mixed Fruit
Pastilles**
(in ¼ lb. and
½ lb. Cartons)

Quality Selection
(in 5 lb. Dri-Dome Jars.)

**Minaret Display Jar.
Mixed Fruit Pastilles.**
(also in attractive Transparent Tubes,
packed 3 Dozen in outer.)

Buttered Brazil Nuts
(in 5 lb. Dri-Dome Jar.)

FROM THE 1926 CATALOGUE.
The fruit pastilles are still in production and a leading brand today,
although now mainly sold in pre-pack bags.

C 730
"ELEGANS"
Oblong Casket
(2 lbs. Kiro Chocolates)
10/-

C 461
"ALPINE BEAUTY"
CASKET
(3 lbs. County Chocolates)
12/-

C 1020
"CAIRN TERRIERS"
(2 lbs. County Chocolates)
8/-

C 1445
"MARQUISE"
S.L. Flanged Box
(1 lb. Kiro Chocolates)
5/-

C 1033
"BARCAROLLE"
Oblong Casket
(1½ lb. Kiro Chocolates)
7/6

C 1024
"ANEMONES"
CASKET
(2 lbs. County Chocolates)
8/-

TYPICAL CHRISTMAS BOXES OF THE 1930's.
The boxes were all made and printed in the factory; the ribbons were tied by hand after the box had been packed.
There were about 50 different picture boxes in the catalogue each Christmas.

59

*Thorneycroft 3 ton van AT 8429,
registered in December 1923.*

*KH 3203, Thorneycroft 3½ ton
van, body built by Barnaby,
registered August 1926.
Note tyres are now pneumatic.*

Dennis 3 ton van KH7881. April 1929.

Needler's

1 lb. OXFORD
(Hard Centres)
CHOCOLATES

Needler's OXFORD Chocolates HARD CENTRES

2/-

1 lb. CHOCOLATE
NUT ASSORTMENT
Fresh nuts in delightful
velvety chocolate.

2/6

1 lb. CAMBRIDGE
(Assorted Centres)
CHOCOLATES

2/-

Needler's

3/-

DORCHESTER
CASKET
Containing 1 lb. Assorted
Chocolates.

1-lb. Tin
WHOLE
BUTTERED
BRAZILS
Fresh, nutritious
nuts, covered with
delightful butter
toffee. Each piece
separately wrap-
ped.

Needler's Whole BUTTERED BRAZILS

2/3

FROM THE 1939 CATALOGUE.
Oxford (Hard centres) & Cambridge (Soft centres) were the two cheaper assortments
introduced to deal with the lack of buying power in the 1930's.

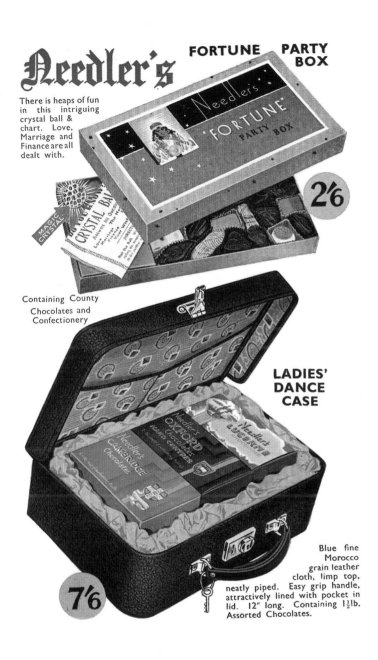

Needler's

FORTUNE PARTY BOX

There is heaps of fun in this intriguing crystal ball & chart. Love, Marriage and Finance are all dealt with.

2/6

Containing County Chocolates and Confectionery

LADIES' DANCE CASE

Blue fine Morocco grain leather cloth, limp top, neatly piped. Easy grip handle, attractively lined with pocket in lid. 12" long. Containing 1½lb. Assorted Chocolates.

7/6

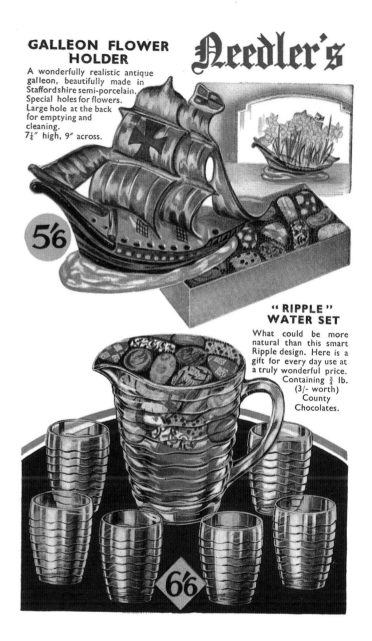

GALLEON FLOWER HOLDER

A wonderfully realistic antique galleon, beautifully made in Staffordshire semi-porcelain. Special holes for flowers. Large hole at the back for emptying and cleaning.
7¼" high, 9" across.

5/6

Needler's

"RIPPLE" WATER SET

What could be more natural than this smart Ripple design. Here is a gift for every day use at a truly wonderful price. Containing ¾ lb. (3/- worth) County Chocolates.

6/6

FROM THE 1939 CATALOGUE.
Four of the novelty types of packaging needed to sell at Christmas in the 1930's; tea sets,
water jugs, cases and even clocks were used. Often the chocolates were only a small proportion of the total price.

*Thorneycroft showvan,
about 1930.
Note glass clerestorey roof to
give daylight to interior.*

*Dennis showvan of 1928,
with display window
built into the side.
Photograph taken in the
Territorial Barracks yard,
Park Street.*

Van display for a pageant. Date unknown.
In front of the Institution, Albion Street.

*Thorneycroft 5 ton van
RH 4019, in 1931. The vehicles
have now changed to a less
primitive look, with large
pneumatic tyres, but the speed is
still limited to 20 m.p.h.
Frank White driving.*

*Fordson 2 ton van, RH 8587
in November 1933.
The speed is now shown as
30 m.p.h.*

Fordson model 18F, 2 1/2 ton van of 1936, with a period streamlined body, for local deliveries.
This is on the company sports field with the factory behind.

The same Fordson delivering, probably in Bridlington. Mr. J.W. Pullen carrying the goods.

To complete the pictures of vans, a 1953 Bedford, PRH 964, with bodywork by Barnaby. This was typical of the large fleet used up to 1965.

One of many pan rooms; this was where the ingredients were cooked for boiled sweets.
There are three Eureka vacuum cookers visible, which pumped the sugar syrup under vacuum around a heated pipe, carrying superheated steam.
By modern standards the area looks very messy, especially as this would be a posed photograph.

Toffee and caramel centre production.
Toffee has been rolled and allowed to cool on the slabs to the left. The cutting machines are on the right, with overhead belt drive, and the finished trays are been inspected in the centre.

The finishing end of the main boiled sweet production. The finished product is on tables, awaiting movement to jar packing.

Chocolate enrobing. The girls are lining-up caramel and nougat centres before they go through the curtain of chocolate which will cover each sweet. Modern plant is very similar, but the machines are much wider, and the feed is automatic.

*Hand-wrapping chocolates
and toffees.
This was soon to be replaced by
the new machinery for wrapping
all sweets.*

*Chocolate packing.
This shows the large, light
working areas in the new factory
building. There is still no
mechanical help in moving
product or boxes, the chocolates
being taken by hand from the
open trays and hand-packed
into boxes which were moved
along the packing line by hand.
Over 70 girls visible
in this room.*

Carton packing.
The girls are folding the cartons from the flat,
then packing them & covering with cellophane.

Inspecting chocolate soldiers.

Box making.
This is the top floor of the
factory, with skylights.
A fair degree of mechanisation
is evident here for folding and
gluing the boxes.
Mr. Batten, the manager is
behind the front machine.

Nut cracking.
Cracking Brazil nuts with hammers.
This must have been the most boring job in the place, but the girls look cheerful.

1926; cleaning of returned glass jars and lids.
The bottles are being washed at the back. All the girls in the foreground are cleaning the aluminium lids; note the inserted perforated discs at the front of the picture; these contained a paper pad to keep the contents dry.

*Another view of the box-making department.
Board being cut on the left; the machine in the foreground is a very early example of one to wrap fancy paper round the card box.*

The accounts office, February 28th at 11.55. Arthur Wood, the company secertary, at the back on the left.

*General office.
These are the book-keepers,
each looking after a number of
hand-written ledgers. It was
regarded as a man's job.
Mr. Rawson who was in charge
is not visible; he always wore a
bowler hat.*

*This is known as "Girls'
Gymnastic Class;" as far as I
know this was a voluntary
organisation, along with the
other games clubs.*

1925. Handpiping department. Chocolates for assortments were individually decorated with thick chocolate on the slabs in the foreground, using paper piping bags, which the girls in the front can be seen holding.

Loading a van in the yard. A human chain would pass the jars into the van, which was fitted with shelves. (Damaged glass negative).

1926. The factory dining room. Obviously a very popular eating place. I estimate about 300 girls in this picture.

Fred Elwell of Beverley painted this picture of the factory dining room in 1924, and it was shown at the Wembley Empire Exhibition in 1925.
As a result of seeing this the Prince of Wales asked to visit the factory.
The painting was unfortunately destroyed, and this copy is taken from a newspaper photograph.

Chocolate making; refiners on the left, to remove any large particles after the basic mix had been through the milling machines on the right.

Visit by Edward, Prince of Wales, 14 October 1926. The Prince with Fred Needler in the factory yard.

The Prince of Wales leaves the factory.
A good view of Bournemouth Street and the factory entrance,
with the new factory in the background.

"Fred Needler conducting community singing, in 1927", according to a note on the back of the photograph.
He is standing on a cart which also has the piano on it. As he has his hat in his left hand, and the pianist is wearing a hat, and many of the girls have outdoor coats on, I think this must be Christmas carols in the factory yard during a lunch break.

Fred Needler's house, Ivydene, in Park Avenue.
This is now a residential home.

The football team in 1912.
Back row; Alfred Thorpe; George Atkinson; J.W. Douglas; E.G. Ross; John Burstall.
Middle row; R.T. Higgins; W. Brockbank; Harry Stow; H. Spence; Frank Melles; Fred Needler.
Front row; Fred Twell; M. Rochester; George Wokes; Tom Blanchard; A.P. Smith.
Seated; W. Chapman; W. Pearson.
Nearly everyone on this photograph spent all his working life with the company;
Mr. Douglas and Mr. Ross both had sons who also joined the company.

NEEDLER'S (LTD.) CRICKET CLUB - - SEASON 1926.

WINNERS OF LUMLEY CUP (1926) AND NATIONAL RADIATOR CHALLENGE BOWL (1926).

			Mr. P. Lazenby, *Director.*			
Mr. A. P. Needler, *Director*	J. Grassam, *Treasurer.*	E. S. Abbott,	P. E. Batten,	H. Curtis,	E. T. Blanshard,	
						Mr. C. P. Thorpe,
T. S. Holyman,	J. T. Burstall, *Director.*	G. Hardy, *Capt.*	Mr. F. Needler, *Managing Director.*	J. G. Sugdon, *Vice-Capt.*	J. Horsfield,	J. Yull,
W. Freeman.						A. P. Smith.

Trophies—Needlers Challenge Cup.   Radiator Challenge Bowl.   Lumley Cup.

83

1925 newspaper advertisement for Melsa chocolates.

A 1-lb. box of *Melsa* Chocolates. Price 5/3.

The eighth Coupon! — now for my FREE CARTON!

Miss Kathleen Singer, who won the "Yorkshire Evening News" and Scala Theatre Beauty Quest, says:—

"Here is the last coupon I need for my free carton! It is so delightful to think that just because I buy NEEDLER'S delicious Chocolates I can get a free Carton every time I have the coupons. I think it is a great idea."

FREE CARTON in exchange for 4 1-lb., 8 ½-lb. or 16 ¼-lb. coupons or mixed coupons of equal value. At all Confectioners.

Ask also for NEEDLER'S Safety First BRONCHIAL PASTILLES In 3d.Packets or loose 1/-qtr.

Needler's
COUNTY CHOCOLATES

NEEDLER'S LTD., HULL, ENGLAND.

There are no better!

There are no better Chocolates than NEEDLER'S.

Millions of people know exactly why.

Because NEEDLER'S are made from the best grades of cocoa bean, the finest sugar, and contain the most delicious centres conceivable.

It is a rare tribute to the *quality* of NEEDLER'S Chocolates that

1,850,000 boxes are packed and sold each year.

Everywhere you go you see them—in the hands of people who discriminate. Red boxes, blue boxes, purple boxes, each containing a delightful assortment.

Ask for NEEDLER'S *Melsa* Assortment in the Purple box ½ lb., 1 lb., 2 lb., or 4 lb. There are no better.

Needler's
MELSA CHOCOLATES
AT YOUR USUAL CONFECTIONERS

Manufactured by NEEDLER'S LTD., HULL. If you cannot obtain these chocolates easily, please drop a card to the above address.

Newspaper advertisement for County Chocolates, 1925.

Box of County chocolates about 1925.

*1935 newspaper advertisement for 2 penny bars
of Kreema chocolate.*

Fred Needler distributing wedding presents in 1926.
Mrs. F. Needler seated in the front.

HULL DAILY MAIL 30 September 1932. Front page headline on Fred Needler's death.

Y. SEPTEMBER 30, 1932

REGISTERED AT THE GENERAL POST OFFICE AS A NEWSPAPER

ONE PENNY

HULL LOSES A WORTHY CITIZEN

MR FRED NEEDLER

GENEROUS, SELF-MADE MAN PASSES TO HIS REST

FOLLOWING an active career in which he gained the esteem of thousands of Hull people and the love of his employees, the death occurred early this morning at Ivydene, Park-avenue, Hull, of Mr Fred Needler, founder, chairman and managing director of Needlers, Ltd., the well-known confectionery manufacturers of this city.

Mr Needler was 67, and it was with feelings of general regret, not only to himself but to his numerous friends and employees, that his illness of recent times perforced his retirement from active association with the firm.

The offices he held in connection with local institutions were high and numerous. At one time he was president of the local branch of the League of Nations Union, and at the time of his death he was a vice-president. He was also a vice-president of the Musical Festival Competitions.

He was associated with the inauguration of the Hull Community Council, and was an ex-chairman of the North-Eastern District of the Manufacturing Confectioners' Alliance.

to about fifty and from these the directorate of the present company were chosen.

On November 14, 1902, the firm changed its title to Messrs Fred Needler Ltd., but, in turn, Spring-street became too small for the growing activity of the firm and it was necessary to go further out, where sufficient land could be obtained to allow of extensions

MR FRED NEEDLER

SOVIET ORDERS
Over £400,000 from British Firms

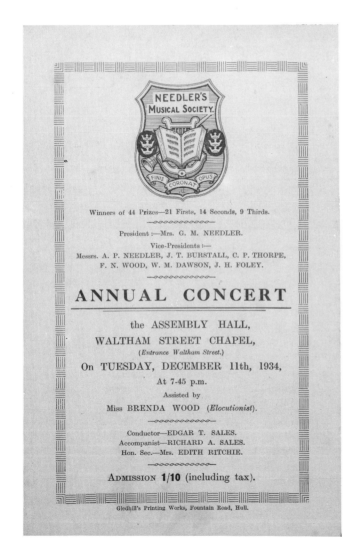

Concert programme cover for the Musical Society in 1934. The programme comprised part songs, madrigals, Christmas carols, and humorous recitations by Brenda Wood.

Easter eggs 1937.
A posed group showing packing of eggs, with a chocolate display piece in the middle.
Directors J.T. Burstall and C.P. Thorpe at the back.

1935. Display jars at a trade show. These giant jars were face-packed by building up each layer of sweets from the bottom and holding them against the glass with wads of paper inside the jar. The actual jars were made as a base with a lid and a cylindrical centre section.

A very large and over-decorated easter egg in 1937.
These were made for display in a shop window, and were usually donated to a local hospital.

The factory at the time of writing; the view from Sculcoates Lane.
The stream is the Barmston & Beverley land drain; the 1916 factory is at the back with the new office building in front.

The factory at the time of writing; from Clough Road.
The land up to Clough Road used to be all fields except for the Sculcoates electricity power station cooling tower, which was built on the company cricket field in 1944, and demolished in 1980. The YEB now have used most of the area up to the railway line, which still exists to serve the Eastern Docks.